GRACE IN ALL ITS GLORY

AN EASTER MUSICAL FOR EVERY CHOIR

ARRANGED AND ORCHESTRATED BY

CAMP KIRKLAND

EXCEL SERIES

lillenas.com

Litho in U.S.A.

Contents

Alleluia, Christ Is Risen

Words and Music by
PHIL MEHRENS
Arr. by Camp Kirkland

13
The Word of life is si - lent in the grave. The Son of God
Bm A Dsus D Bm A
16
a - waits the dawn; His an - gel comes and
G D Bm A
18
cresc.
rolls the stone a - way. He ris - es,
cresc.
Dsus D G A G/B A/C♯
cresc.

21
CD: 2
f
He ris - es. Al - le -
G/B A G/B A/C♯ D
24
lu - ia, al - le - lu - ia; Christ is ris - en from the
G D G/D D A Bm G
f
27
dead. Al - le - lu - ia, al - le - lu - ia; Christ is
A G D G/D D A Bm

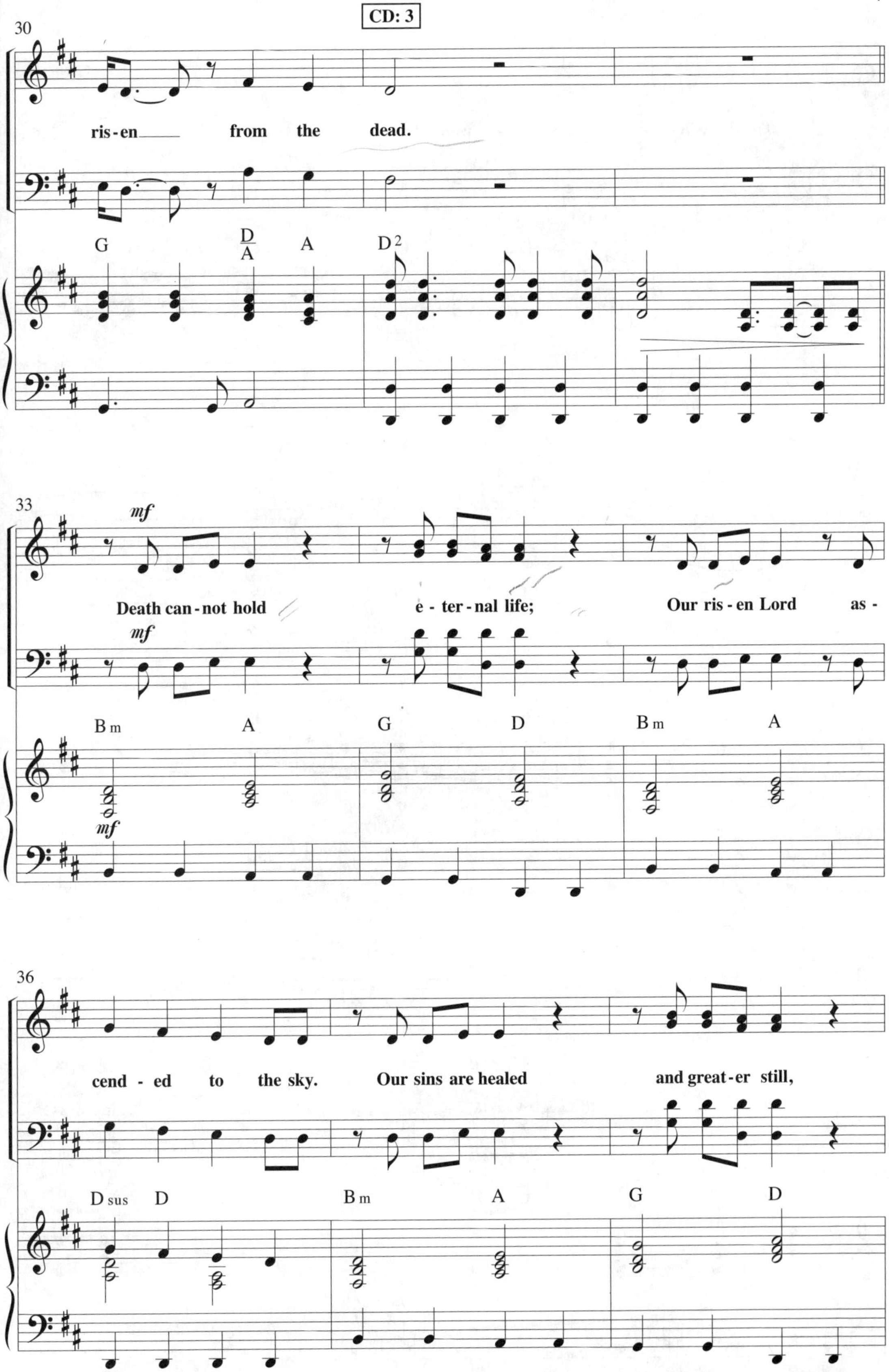
CD: 3
30
ris - en from the dead.
G
D/A
A
D2
33
mf
Death can - not hold e - ter - nal life; Our ris - en Lord as -
mf
Bm
A
G
D
Bm
A
mf
36
cend - ed to the sky. Our sins are healed and great - er still,
Dsus
D
Bm
A
G
D

39

cresc.

The day will dawn when those who hope in Christ ___ will ___

cresc.

Bm A D sus D G A

42

CD: 4

rise, ___ we will ___ rise. ___

G/B A/C♯ G/B A G/B A/C♯

cresc.

45

f

Al - le - lu - ia, al - le -

f

D B♭ E♭/G E♭ A♭ E♭ A♭/E♭ E♭

f

47
lu - ia; Christ is ris-en from the dead. Al - le -
B♭ Cm A♭ B♭
50
CD: 5
lu - ia, al - le - lu - ia; Christ is ris-en from the
A♭ E♭ A♭/E♭ E♭ B♭ Cm A♭ E♭/B♭ B♭
53
dead. Al - le - lu - ia, al - le -
E♭ Csus F/A F N.C. B♭ F N.C.

55
lu - ia; Christ is ris - en from the
C Dm N.C. B♭
57
dead. Al - le - lu - ia, al - le - lu - ia; Christ is
CD: 6 1st time
C B♭ F B♭/F F C Dm
60
ris - en from the dead. Al - le dead. Christ is
1 (to pg. 9, meas. 54)
2
B♭ F/C C
1 F (to pg. 9, meas. 54)
2 F

(Without music)

NARRATOR: Alleluia! He is risen indeed! He's alive, and we find our life in Him! We have so much to celebrate today!

Two thousand years ago, the crowds welcomed Jesus into Jerusalem shouting, "Hosanna! God's salvation is here! Blessed is He who comes in the name of the Lord!" And today, we echo their cries. We long for Jesus to come again, and reign forever! *(Music begins)*

Forever Reign (Medley)

includes

Forever Reign
Christ the Lord Is Risen Today
Alleluia! Alleluia!

Words and Music by
MARTY FUNDERBURK
and STEVEN R. ADAMS
Arr. by Camp Kirkland

10
Rule o - ver all the earth as Lord of ev - 'ry -
F C/E F B♭/D F/C Dm/B♭
13
thing. Let all cre - a - tion sing ho -
Csus C F/C C♯°7
16
san - na to Your name. For - ev - er
D4/2 Dm C/E Dm/F D/F♯ Gm F/A B♭6

CD: 8
reign, Je - sus
F/C G9/C Csus C7
reign.
mf
Wel - come our Mes -
D♭ D♭2 D♭ D♭2 D♭ E♭/D♭
si - ah, all Jer - ru - sal - em. A -
A♭/C D♭ E♭/D♭ A♭/C

CD: 9

28

rise, Daught - er of Zi - on, come, wor - ship Him.

B♭m7 | A♭/C | D♭M7

31

f

For - ev - er reign, our

f

C sus | C | C 4/2 | C/B♭ | F/A | B♭

f

34

long a - wait - ed King. Rule o - ver

Dm/B | C sus | C | C sus/D | C/E | F | C/E | F

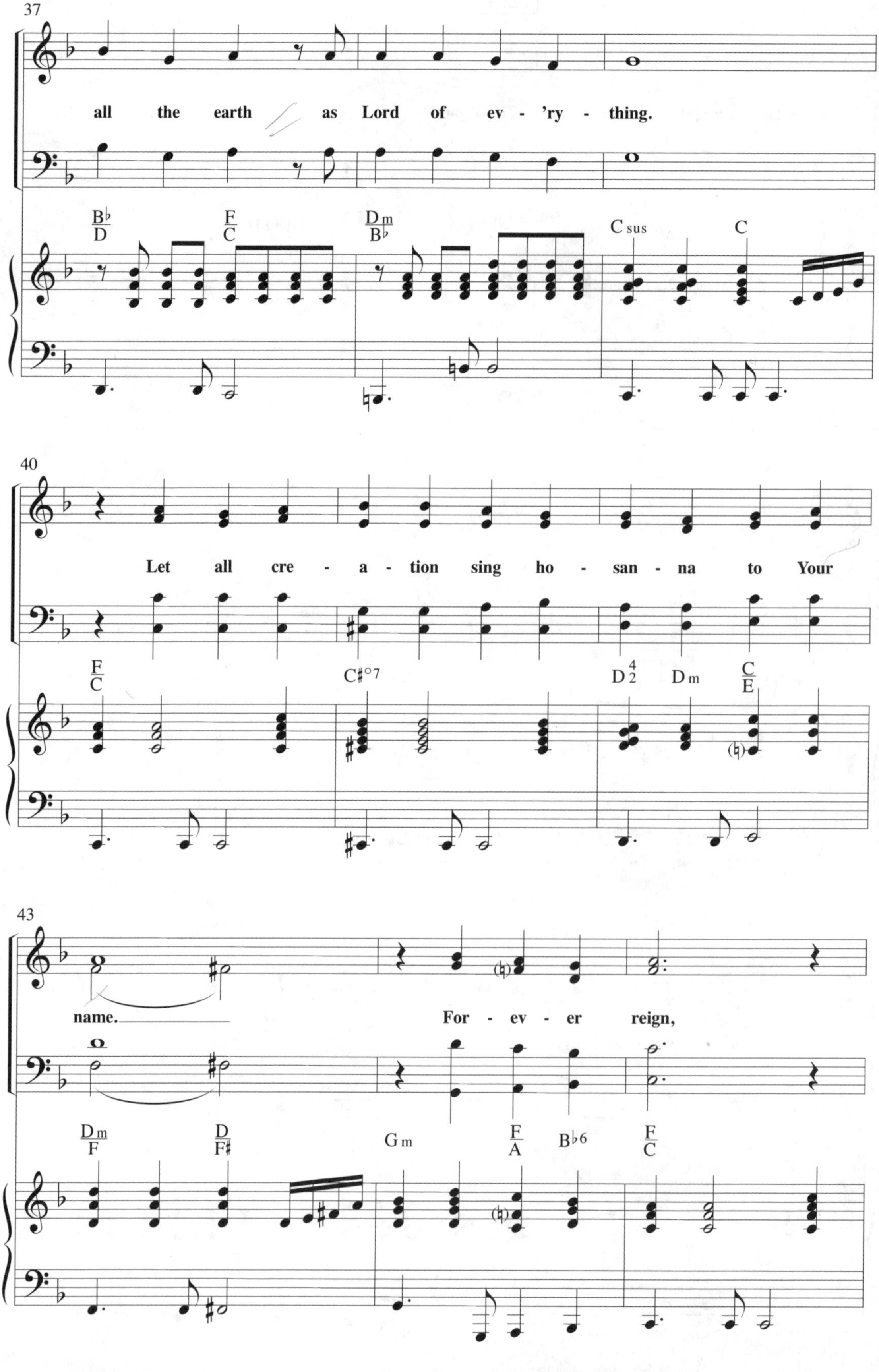

37

all the earth as Lord of ev - 'ry - thing.

B♭/D F/C Dm/B♭ Csus C

40

Let all cre - a - tion sing ho - san - na to Your

F/C C♯°7 D4/2 Dm C/E

*Words by CHARLES WESLEY; Music *Lyra Davidica*. Arr.

55
an - gels say:
Al - le - lu - ia!
Dm7 C C/G G C Csus/D C/E Dm7 C F/A C/G G7 C
58
Raise your joys and tri - umphs high.
Al - le -
G Gsus/A G/B G C/E G C G G/B Am7
61
lu - ia!
Sing, ye heav'ns, and earth, re - ply:
G/D D7 G G/F C/E C F Dm7 F/G G7

CD: 11
64
Al - le - lu - ia!
C G7/D C/E C F G7/D C/E Dm/F C/G G7 C Bb/C C C/Bb
67
For - ev - er reign, our long a - wait - ed King.
F/A Bb Dm/B
70
Rule o - ver all the earth as
Csus C Csus/D C/E F C/E F Bb/D F/C

73
Lord of ev - 'ry - thing.
Let all cre -
Dm
B♭
C sus
C
F
C
76
a - tion sing ho - san - na to Your name.
C♯°7
D 4 2
Dm
C
E
Dm
F
D
F♯
79
CD: 12
For - ev - er reign,
Je - sus
Gm
F
A
B♭6
F
C
G 9
C
C sus
C 7

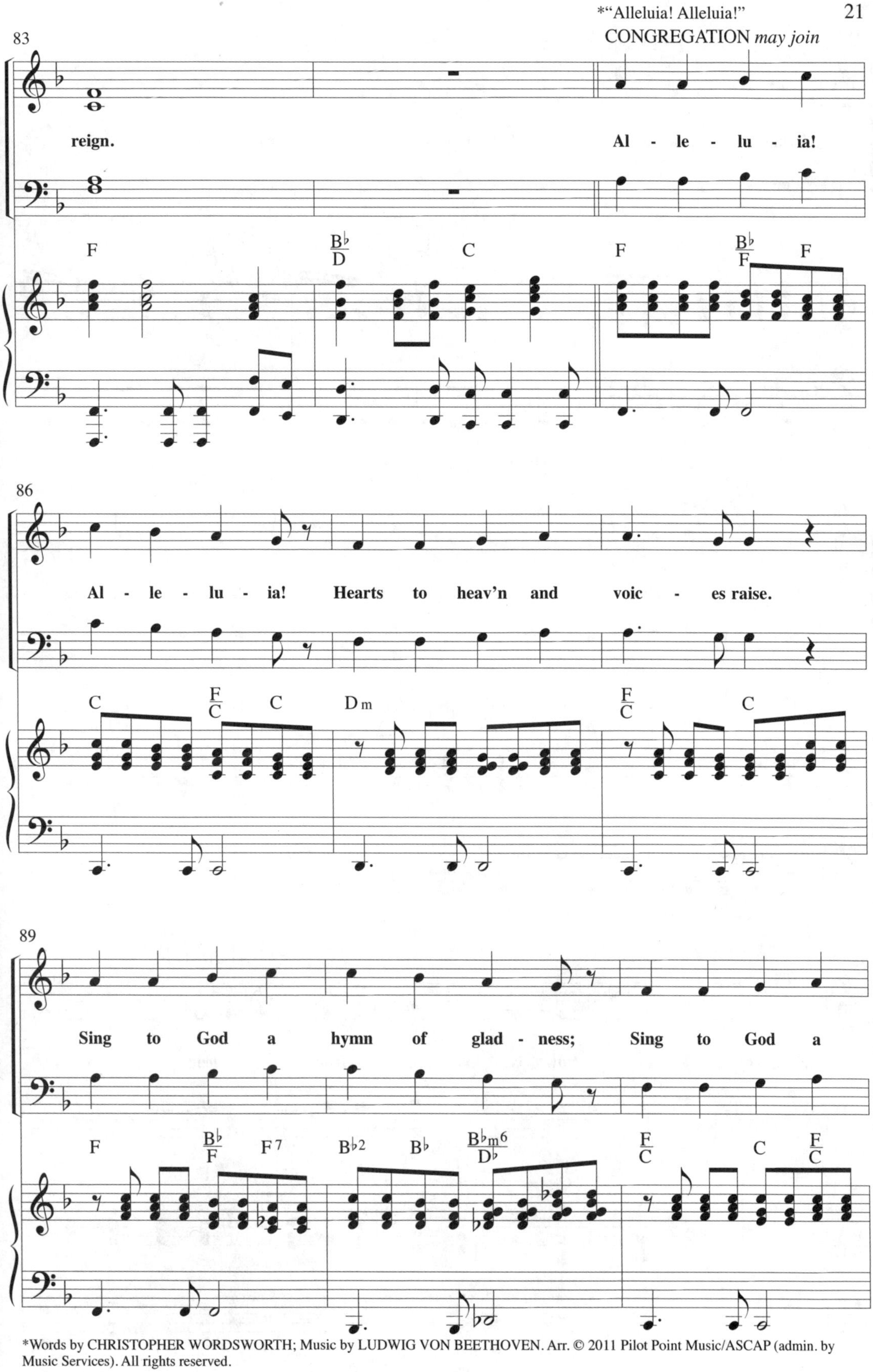
*"Alleluia! Alleluia!"
CONGREGATION *may join*
83
reign.
Al - le - lu - ia!
F
B♭/D
C
F
B♭/F
F
86
Al - le - lu - ia! Hearts to heav'n and voic - es raise.
C
F/C
C
Dm
F/C
C
89
Sing to God a hymn of glad - ness; Sing to God a
F
B♭/F
F7
B♭2
B♭
B♭m6/D♭
F/C
C
F/C

*Words by CHRISTOPHER WORDSWORTH; Music by LUDWIG VON BEETHOVEN. Arr. © 2011 Pilot Point Music/ASCAP (admin. by Music Services).

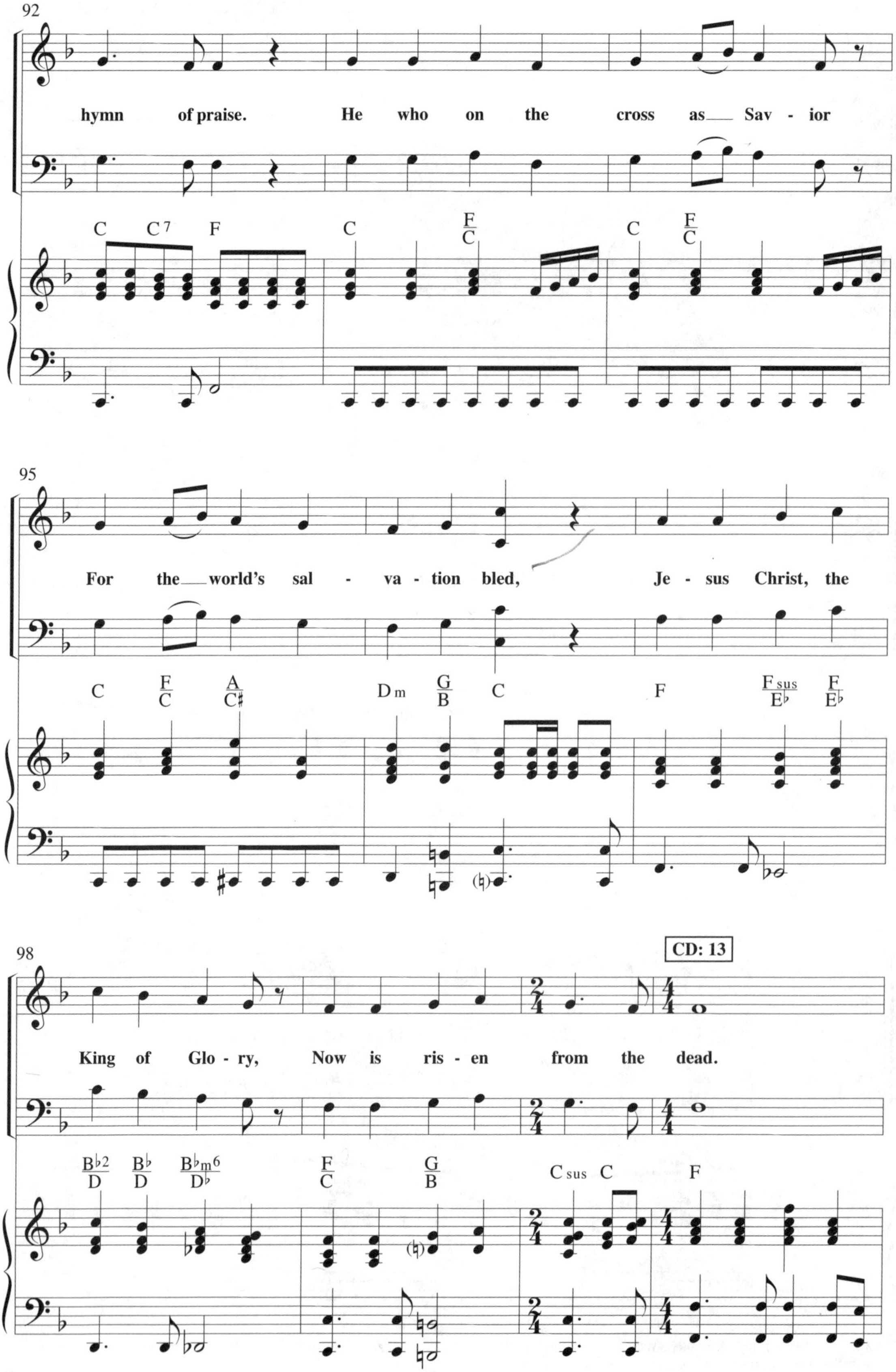

92
hymn of praise. He who on the cross as Sav - ior
C C7 F C F/C C F/C
95
For the world's sal - va - tion bled, Je - sus Christ, the
C F/C A/C♯ Dm G/B C F Fsus/E♭ F/E♭
98
CD: 13
King of Glo - ry, Now is ris - en from the dead.
B♭2/D B♭/D B♭m6/D♭ F/C G/B Csus C F

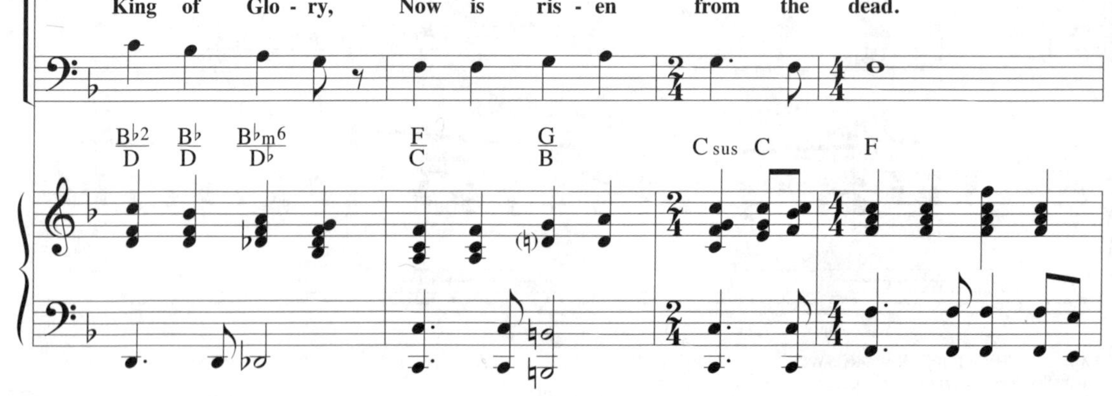

102
rit.
Broader ♩ = ca. 96
Now the i - ron bars are bro - ken;
C/D D C/D D G Am/G G Bm/D Am/D G/D D♯°7
rit.
broader
105
Christ from death to life is born–
Glo - rious life, and
Em B7/D♯ Em/D Em/C♯ D7 G Am/G G7
108
life im - mor - tal
On this res - ur - rec - tion morn.
CM7 C6 Cm6/E♭ G/D Am/D G/D Dsus D Gsus/D G

111
Christ has tri - umphed, and we con - quer
Christ has tri - umphed, and we con - quer
D
G/D
D
G/D
113
By His mighty - y en - ter - prise;
D
B7/D♯
Em
A/C♯
D
115
We with Him to life e - ter - nal By His res - ur -
G
G7sus/F
G7/F
C2/E
C/E
Cm6/E♭
G/D
A/C♯

118
rec - tion rise. We with Him to life e - ter - nal
D sus D G sus/D G G7sus/F G7/F C M7/E C6/E C m6/E♭
121
cresc.
By His res - ur - rec - tion rise.
ff
change voice
G/D A/C♯ D sus D G G sus/D G G sus/D
124
G G sus/D G G sus/D G

In the Shadow of the Cross

TRACY BARKER and
ISAAC WATTS

TRACY BARKER and
RALPH E. HUDSON
Arr. by Camp Kirkland

8
Know-ing all that I have done Do I dare to e-ven come?
D (no3)
B
D (no3)
G

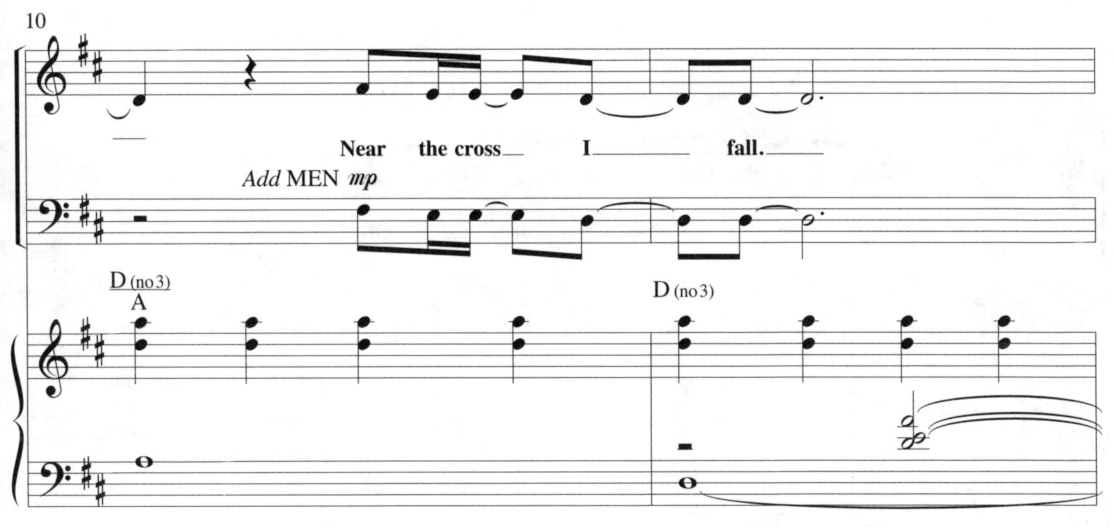
10
Near the cross I fall.
Add MEN mp
D (no3)
A
D (no3)

12
No more strength to e-ven crawl,
D (no3)
B m7

14

Still my faith is un - de-terred; Know-ing I do not de-serve

B m7 G 2

16

CD: 15

To be near the cross at all.

A sus D (no3)

Ped.

18

mf

In the shad - ow of the cross Hum-bly,

D (no3) D/F♯ G B m7 A sus A D/F♯

mf

21
I sur-ren - der all;
Lord, may I be ev - er lost
G B m7 A sus A D/F♯ G B m7
24
CD: 16
In the shad - ow of the cross.
A sus D/F♯ G 2
26
Near the cross I pray,
Near the cross I
G 2 D 2

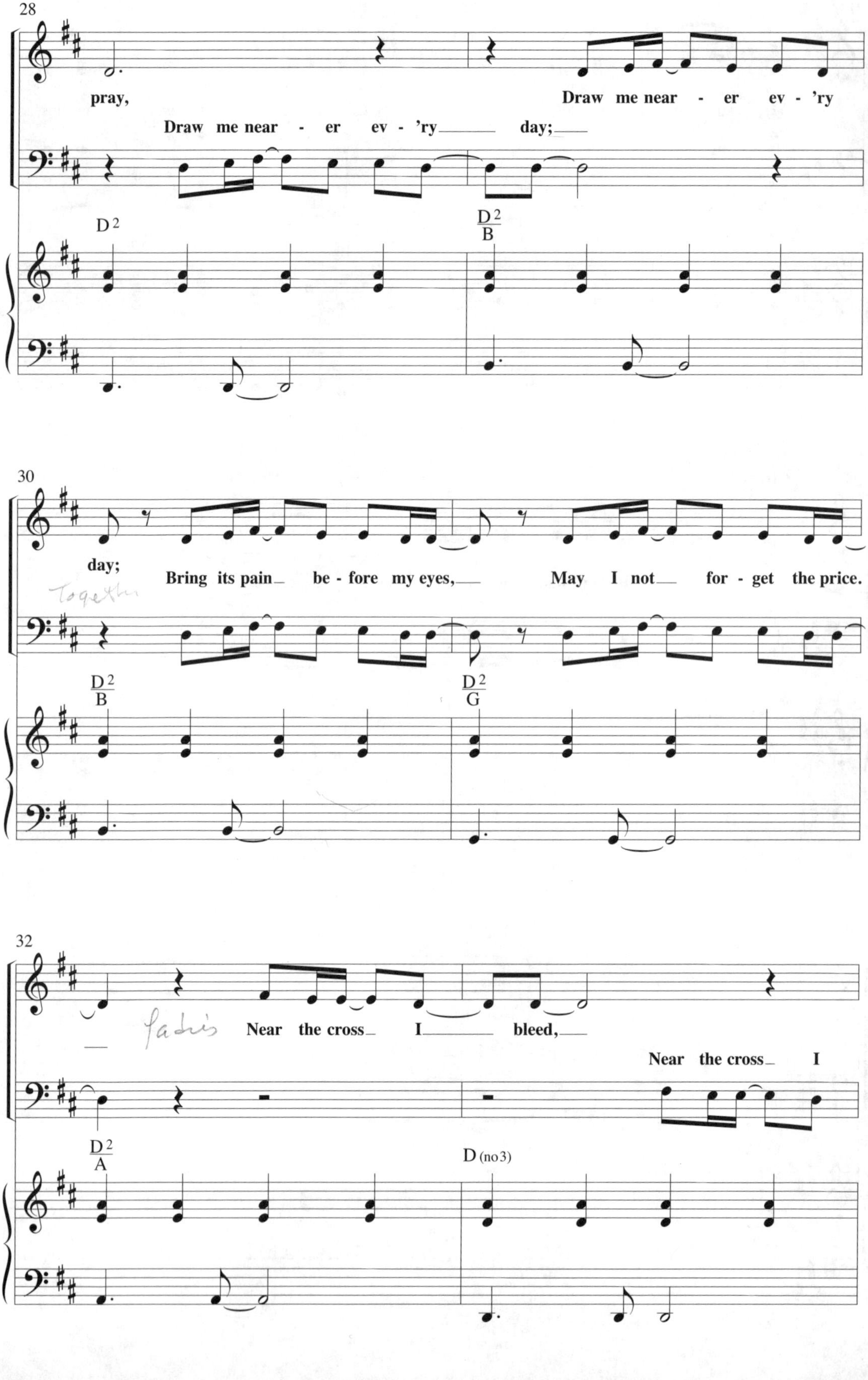

28

pray, Draw me near - er ev - 'ry

Draw me near - er ev - 'ry day;

D2 D2/B

30

day; Bring its pain be - fore my eyes, May I not for - get the price.

Together

D2/B D2/G

34
No more fight - ing, I con - cede;
bleed,
No more fight - ing, I con -
D (no3)
B m7
36
Though my heart is full of fear
Bring - ing all that I hold dear.
cede;
B m7
G 2
38
cresc.
CD: 17
Lay it down and set it free.
cresc.
A sus
D
cresc.

40
f
In the shad - ow of the cross
Hum - bly,
D
D/F♯
G
B m7
A sus
A
43
I sur - ren - der all;
Lord, may I be ev - er lost
46
CD: 18
In the shad - ow of the cross.
G2

48
LADIES unis.
mp
But drops of grief can ne'er re - pay The
G2
D (no3)
D (no3)
C♯
mp
51
debt of love I owe.
Here, Lord, I give my -
Add MEN mp
D (no3)
B
D (no3)
A
D (no3)
G
54
CD: 19
f
self a - way; 'Tis all that I can do.
In the
f
D
F♯
Em7
D
A
A
D
D
F♯
cresc.

57
shad - ow of the cross
Hum - bly, I sur - ren - der all;
G
B m7
A sus
A
D/F♯
G
B m7
f
60
Lord, may I be ev - er lost
A sus
A
D/F♯
G
B m7
62
CD: 20
In the shad - ow of the cross.
A sus
D/F♯
G 2

64
In the shadow of the cross
G2
G
Bm7
66
Where Your grace and mercy fall;
Lord, may
Asus
A
D/F♯
G
Bm7
Asus
A
D/F♯
69
CD: 21
mf
I be ever lost
In the shadow of the
mf
G
Bm7
Asus
D/F♯
dim.

71
LADIES unis.
mp
cross.
Near the cross I'll
G2
mp
73
stay
Though all oth - ers turn a -
D (no3)
75
- way;
Still I mar - vel at Your worth
Add MEN mp
D (no3)
B

(Without music)

NARRATOR: Romans 5:8 says the greatest demonstration of love in history was on that cross . . . that day, “in that while we were still sinners, Christ died for us.” We couldn’t see how desperate we were for the love of God, but God loved us anyway. We were oblivious to our need for grace, but God gave it anyway. *(Music begins)*

They Could Not

Words and Music by
CLAIRE CLONINGER
and RON HARRIS
Arr. by Camp Kirkland

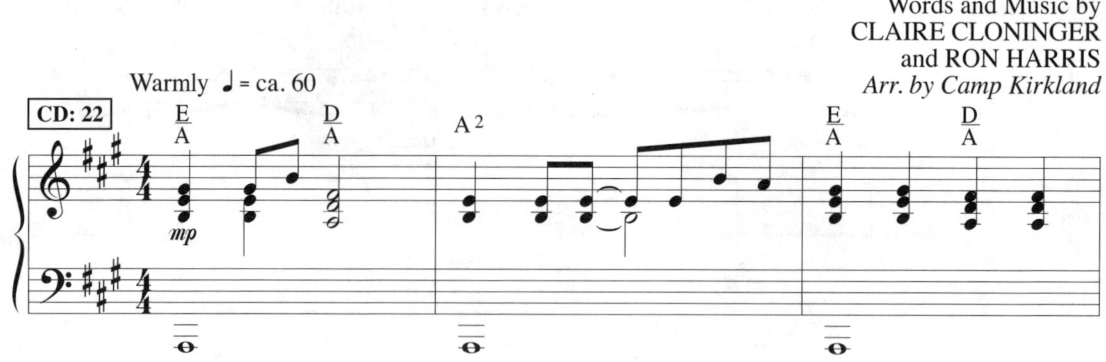

8
hands.
They saw Him calm the sea and
C♯m7/F♯
F♯m7
D M7
10
heal a dy - ing man; They saw but could they real - ly un - der -
A2/C♯
F2/C
F/C
F M7/C
F6/C
CD: 23
12
rit.
a tempo
stand?
They could not, they could
CHOIR unis.
a tempo mp
Oo,
mp
Dm/B
E7sus
E7
A2
C♯m7
rit.
a tempo

15
not, Tho' they tried, they could not. He was
Oo, Oo.
D M7
B m7
D/E
A
A/G
B 9/F♯
D m6/F
18
just a sim - ple car - pen - ter with heal - ing in His hands. But could they
A/E
E/F♯
F♯m7
D M9
D m(M7)
D m6
20
CD: 24
real - ly un - der - stand? They could not.
A 2/E
A/E
D/E
A 2
A

22
They lis - tened to the teach - ing that they
D2/A E/A D/A
24
heard And won - dered at the mys - t'ry of His
A2 A E/A D/A
26
Word. They won - dered what He meant a -
C#m7/F# F#m7 DM7
28
bout a Fa - ther's plan. They heard but could they real - ly un - der -
A2/C# F2/C F/C FM7/C F6/C

30 CD: 25

stand? They could not, they could

CHOIR *unis.* *mp*

They could not,

mp

Here

Dm/B E7sus E7 A2 C♯m7

33

not, Tho' they tried, they could not. They

they could not, they tried, they could not.

DM7 Bm7 D/E A A/G B9/F♯ Dm6/F

36

lis-tened to His teach-ing a-bout a Fa-ther's plan. But could they

A/E E/F♯ F♯m7 DM9 Dm(M7) Dm6

38

real-ly un-der-stand? They could not.

mf

They could

mf

Here

A2/E A/E D/E A2 A

40
CD: 26
So
not.
They could not.
D
A
B♭2
B♭
E♭
B♭
43
fi - nal - ly up - on a rug - ged cross,
They
F
B♭
E♭
B♭
B♭2
B♭
45
killed the Man who would not suf - fer loss.
And
F
B♭
E♭
B♭
F
G
Gm7

47
when at last they took what will - ing - ly He gave, He
E♭M7
B♭2
D
49
CD: 27
died but could they keep Him in the grave.
G♭
D♭
G♭M7
D♭
G♭6
D♭
E♭m6
C
3
51
rit.
a tempo
They could not,
CHOIR unis.
f
They could not, they could
F7sus
B♭2
Dm7

53

they could not, praise God, they could

not, praise God, they could

E♭2 E♭ Cm7 E♭/F B♭ A♭/B♭ B♭

55

not. And when at last they took from Him what

not.

E♭M9 G♭M7/A♭ A♭9 B♭/F F/G Gm

57

will - ing - ly He gave. Could they keep Him in the grave? Could they

All → Here

They could

E♭M7 E♭m(M7) E♭m6 B♭/F

59 CD: 28

keep Him in the grave? Could they keep Him in the grave?

not, they could not.

Gm7 E♭M7 Cm7

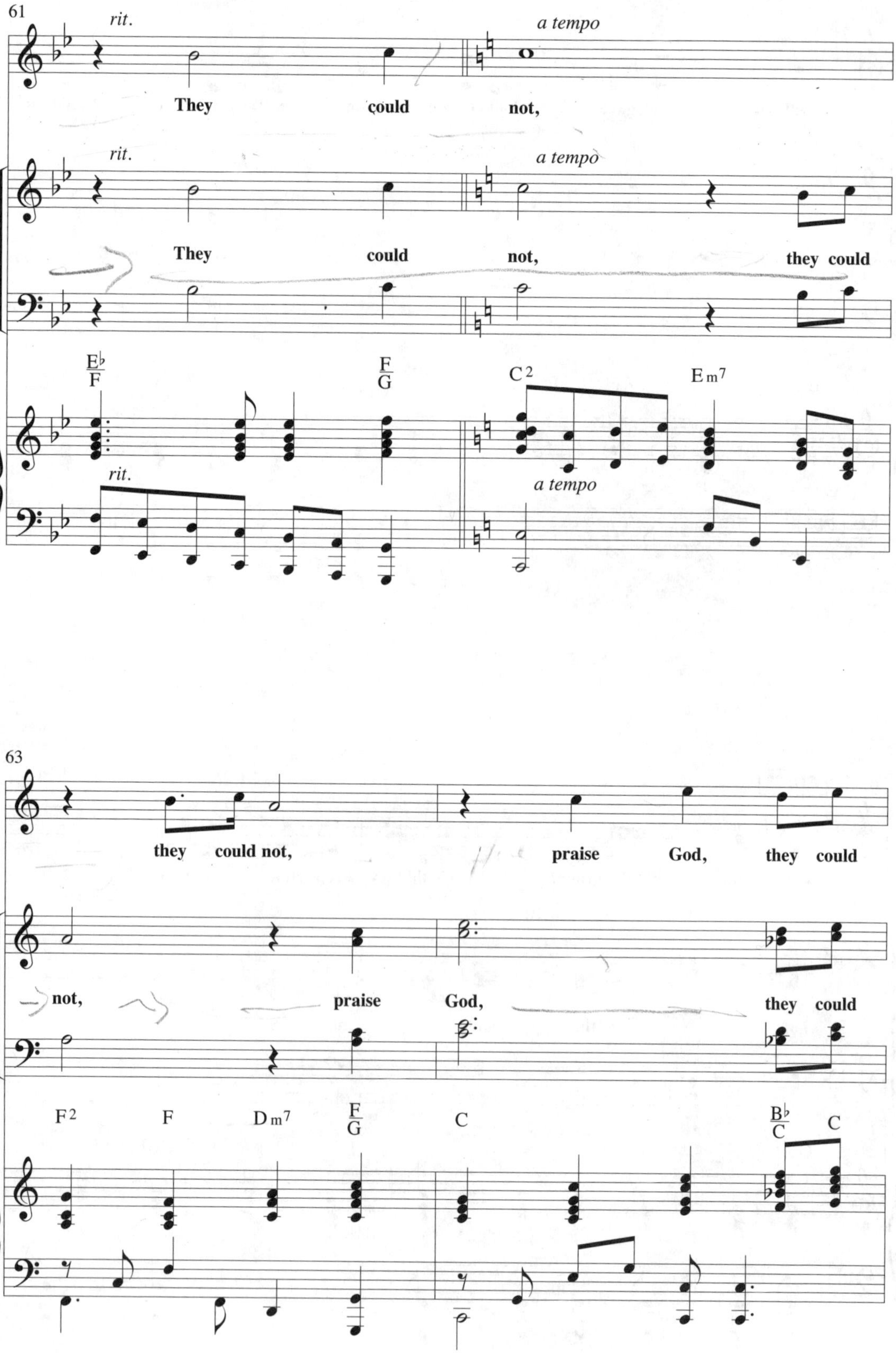

63

they could not, praise God, they could

not, praise God, they could

F2 F Dm7 F/G C B♭/C C

65

not. And when at last they took from Him what

not.

FM9 A♭M7/B♭ B♭9 C/G G/A Am

67 CD: 29

will - ing - ly He gave. Could they keep Him in the grave? Could they

They could

FM7 Fm(M7) Fm6 C/G

69
keep Him in the grave? Could they keep Him in the grave?
not, they could not, they could
Am7
FM7
C/E
E♭°7
71
rit.
They could not!
not, they could not!
Dm7
F/G
Fm/G
C
C/B♭
rit.

(Without music)

NARRATOR: Praise God! Nothing could keep Jesus in the grave that day! The central event in all of human history had taken place, and everyone knew it. The guards at the tomb knew it. The disciples knew it. And soon the whole world would know, Jesus is alive forevermore! *(Music begins)*

When the Stone Rolled Away

Words and Music by
JOEL LINDSEY, JOHN DARIN ROWSEY
and KAREN PECK GOOCH
Arr. by Camp Kirkland

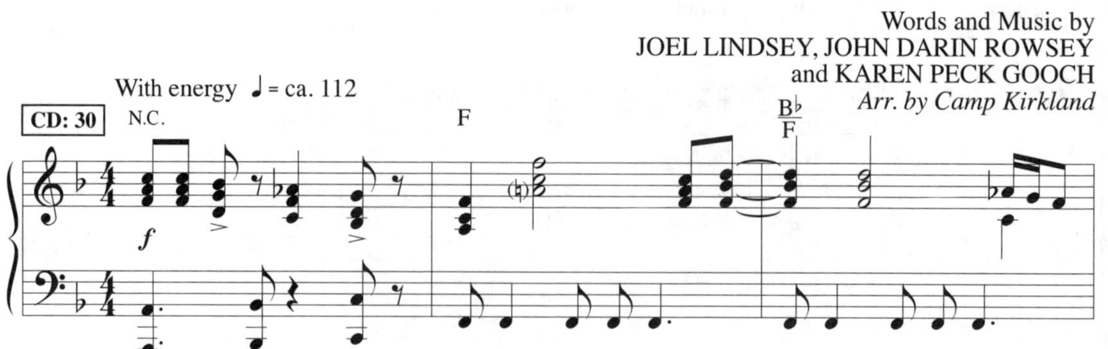

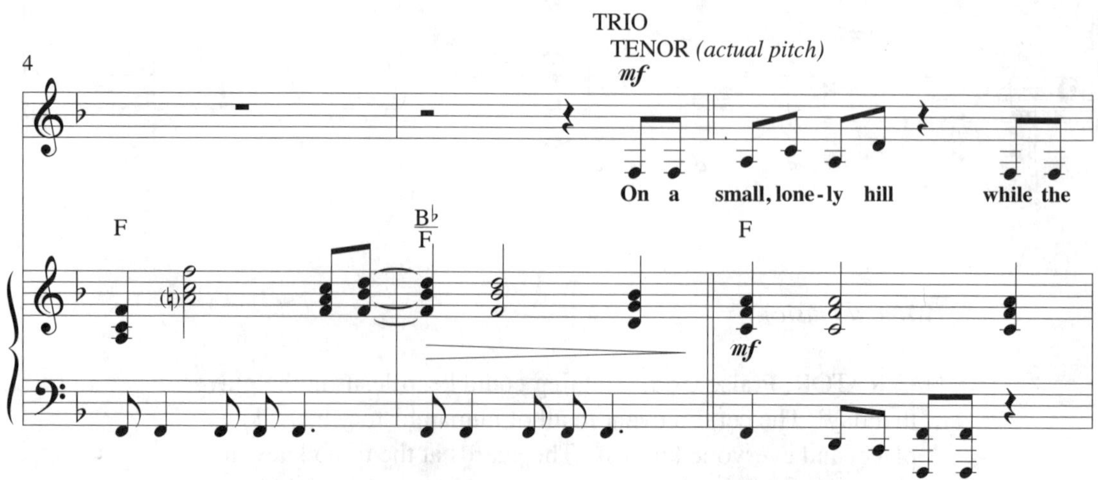

9
SOPRANO
mf
You see, the Lord has been cru - ci - fied
F
Fsus
G
F7
A
A♭
B♭
B♭9

11
TENOR
mf
for ev - 'ry - bod - y to see.
O the
B♭9
F

14
ALTO
mf
tomb must have seemed like the end of a dream For
F

16
CD: 31
SOPRANO
mf
those watch - ing Him hang on the cross.
And ev - 'ry - thing that He
F
F sus
G
F 7
A
18
prom - ised them
just turned in - to loss.
A♭
B♭
B♭9
B♭
C
21
TRIO
f
But on the third day the stone was rolled a - way,
CHOIR parts
f
But on the third day the stone was rolled a - way,
B♭
C
F
C
E

23
The on - ly thing left to find was an emp - ty place.
The on - ly thing left to find was an emp - ty place.
E♭
B♭
D
F
C
E

25
He said, "The vic - t'ry was mine." He had the keys all the time
He said, "The vic - t'ry was mine." He had the keys all the time
E♭
B♭
D
A 7
E

27

to death, hell and the grave___ when the stone___ rolled a - way.___

to death, hell and the grave___ when the stone___ rolled a - way.___

Dm Cm7 B♭ B♭/C

30 **CD: 32**

F B♭/F F

33

ALTO
TENOR
mf

Now the on - ly re - mains of

B♭/F F

35

SOPRANO
ALTO
mf

death and its chains Are the mem - 'ries of the way that it was

F

37

be - fore our Sav - ior rose a - gain

F Fsus/G F7/A A♭/B♭ B♭9

39

TRIO
mf

to give the vic - t'ry to us.

ALTO
TENOR
mf

So when you're

B♭9 F

42
SOPRANO
TENOR
mf
fac - ing de - feat and it's hard to be - lieve You can
F

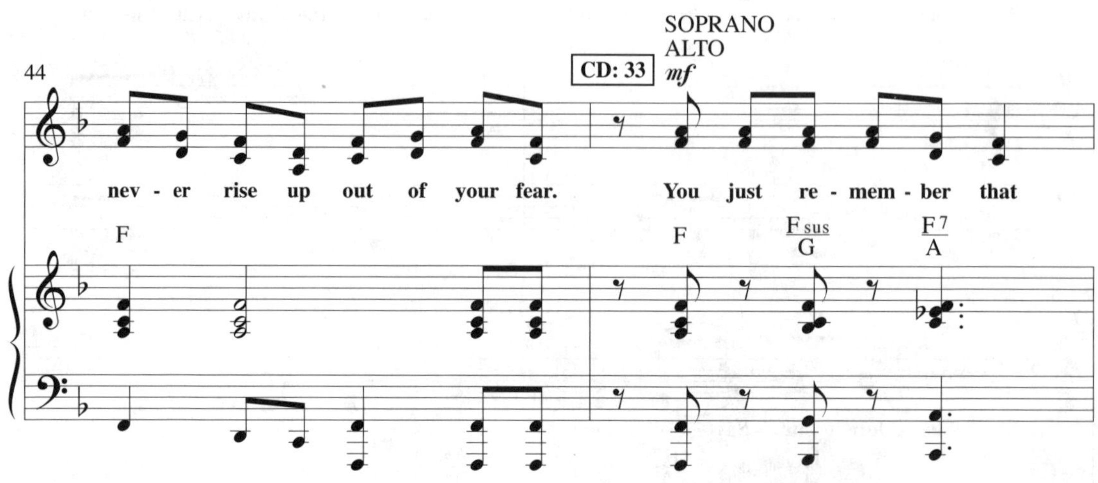
44
CD: 33
SOPRANO
ALTO
mf
nev - er rise up out of your fear. You just re - mem - ber that
F
F
F sus
G
F 7
A

46
TRIO
mf
emp - ty tomb and dry your des - p'rate tears.
A♭
B♭
B♭9

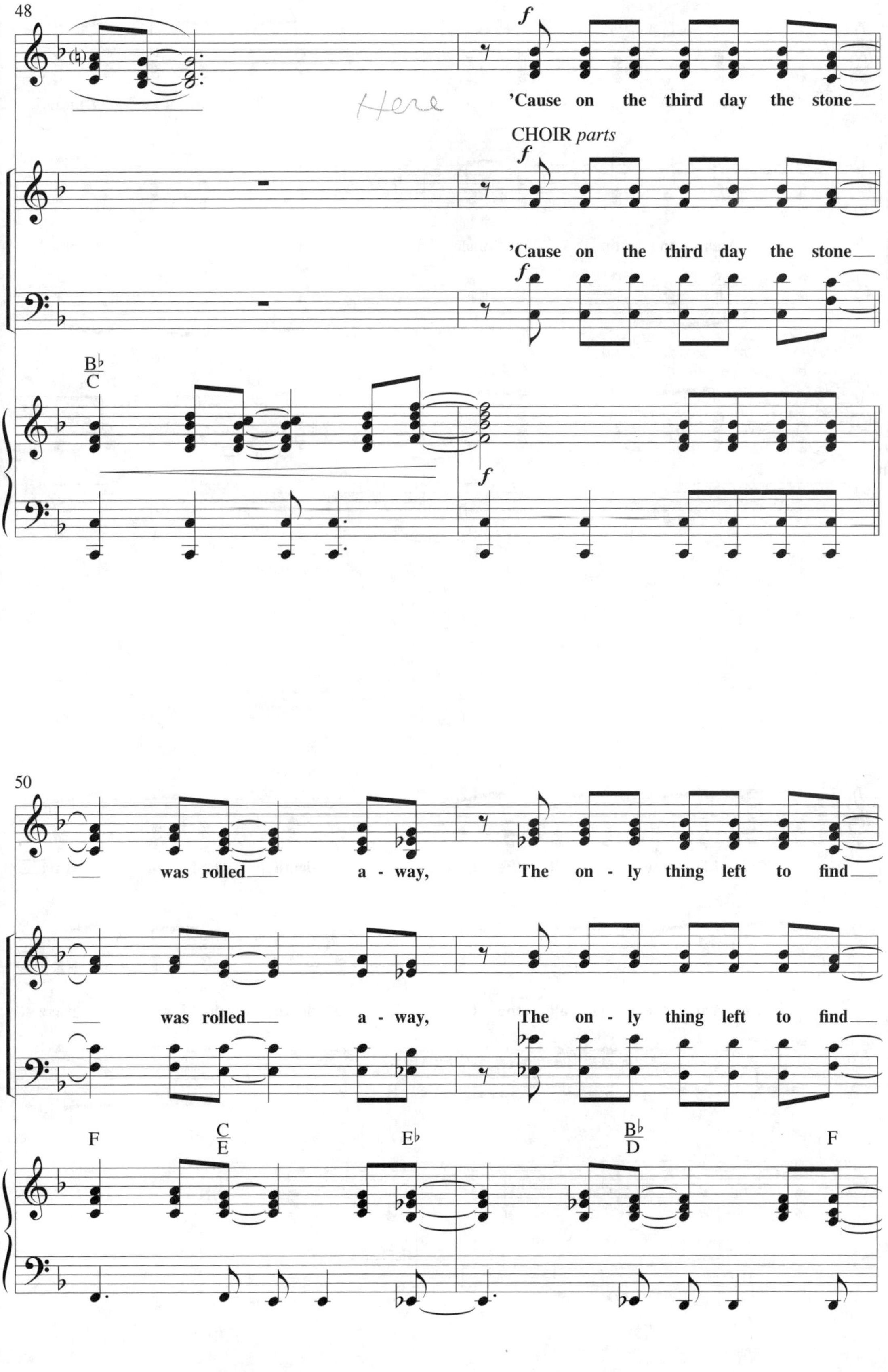

48

f

'Cause on the third day the stone

CHOIR *parts*

f

'Cause on the third day the stone

f

B♭
C

f

52
was an emp - ty place. He said, "The vic - t'ry was mine."
was an emp - ty place. He said, "The vic - t'ry was mine."
F
C
E
E♭
B♭
D
F

54
He had the keys all the time to death, hell and the grave
He had the keys all the time to death, hell and the grave
F
A7
E
Dm
Cm7

56

CD: 34

when the stone rolled a - way.

when the stone rolled a - way.

B♭ | B♭/C

58

E♭2 | B♭/D | A m7/D

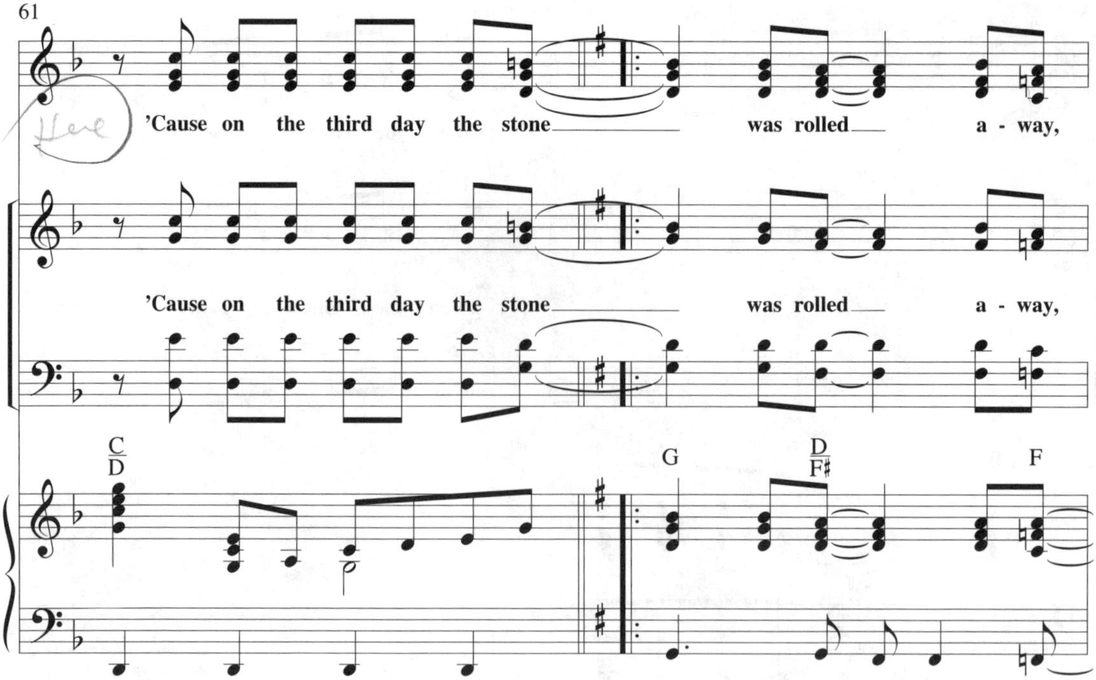
61
Here
'Cause on the third day the stone was rolled a - way,
'Cause on the third day the stone was rolled a - way,
C/D
G
D/F♯
F

63
The on - ly thing left to find was an emp - ty place.
The on - ly thing left to find was an emp - ty place.
F
C/E
G
D/F♯
F

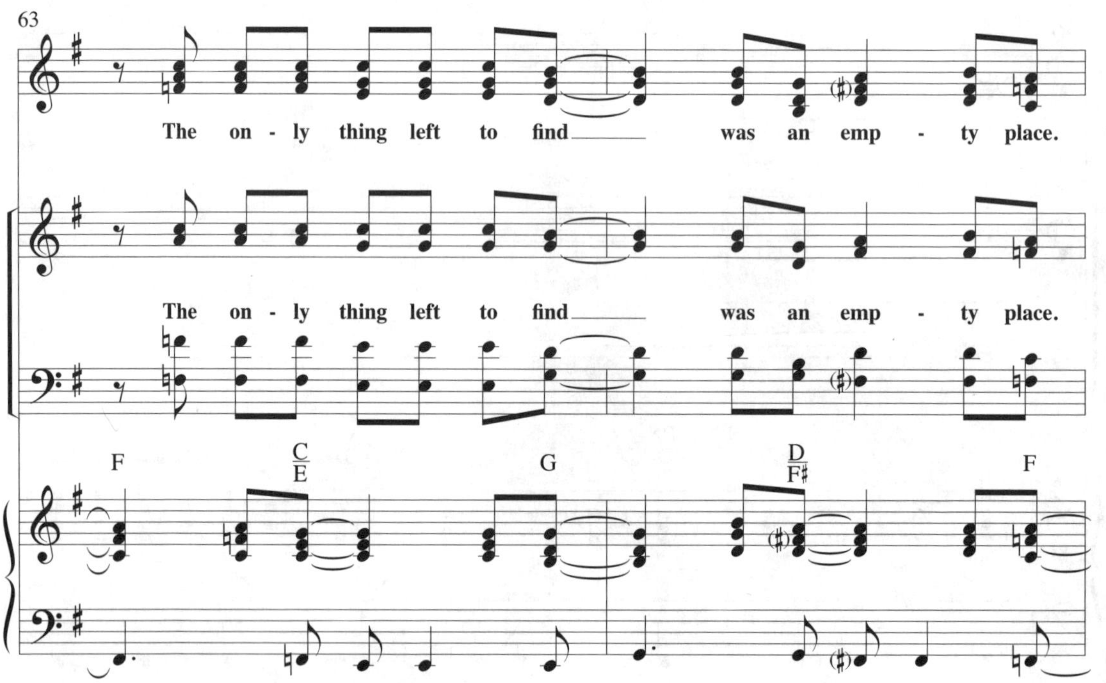

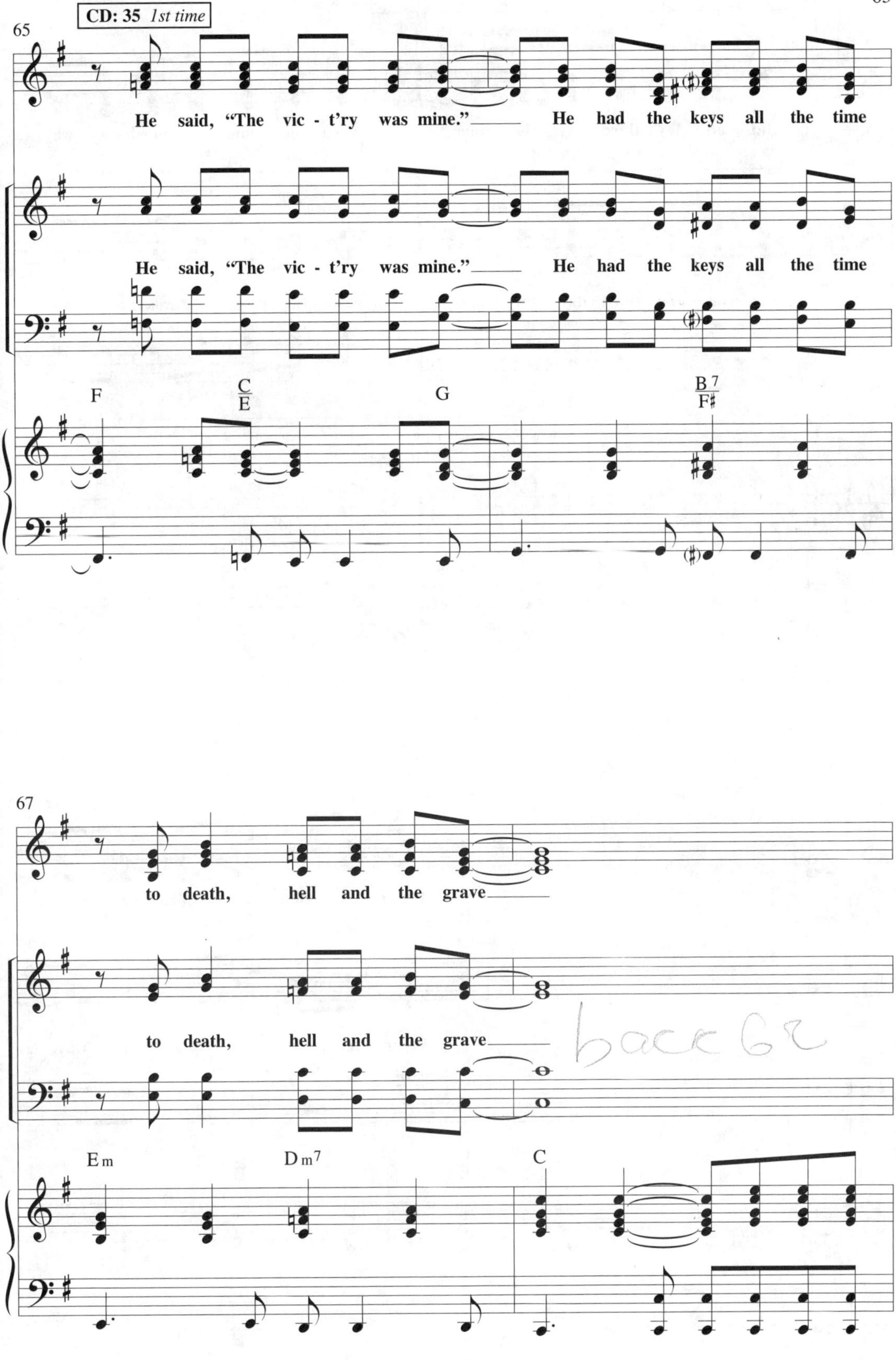

CD: 35 *1st time*

65

He said, "The vic - t'ry was mine."___ He had the keys all the time

He said, "The vic - t'ry was mine."___ He had the keys all the time

F C/E G B7/F♯

69

1 (to pg. 62, meas. 62) 2

But on the third day the stone___ when the stone___ rolled a - way.___

1 (to pg. 62, meas. 62) 2

But on the third day the stone___ when the stone___ rolled a - way.___

1 (to pg. 62, meas. 62) 2

C/D C/D

71

When the stone___ rolled a - way.___

When the stone___ rolled a - way.___

F2 C/E C/D

73

ff

When the stone rolled a - way.

ff

When the stone rolled a - way.

Here

ff

F2

C/E

C/D

Bis.

75

G

ff

The Head That Once Was Crowned with Thorns

Words and Music by
TONY WOOD and
CARL CARTEE
Arr. by Camp Kirkland

CD: 36

Acoustic feel ♩ = ca. 84

B♭ — B♭/A — E♭2/G

mp

4

LADIES *unis.*
mp

The Head that once was crowned with thorns is

E♭2 — B♭ — F/A — Gm

7

crowned with glo - ry now. A roy - al di - a -

E♭ — B♭/D — Fsus — F — B♭ — F/A

CD: 37
10
mf
dem a - dorns the might - y Vic - tor's brow.
The
Add MEN mf
Gm
E♭
F sus
F
B♭
13
high - est place that heav'n af - fords be - longs to Him by
B♭
F
A
Gm
E♭
B♭
D
mf
16
cresc.
right.
Je - sus reigns as Lord of lords, as
cresc.
F sus
F
B♭
F
A
Gm

19
CD: 38
heav'n's e - ter - nal Light.
Once the suf - f'ring
E♭
Fsus
F
B♭
E♭
F
B♭2
22
Ser - vant, now the King to whom we bow.
The
B♭/A
Gm7
E♭
25
Head that once was crowned with thorns is crowned with glo - ry,
B♭
B♭/A
Gm7

28
crowned with glo - ry now.
E♭2
B♭
F
A
31
CD: 39
mf
For the joy that was to come
mf
G m4 7
E♭2
B♭
F
A
G m
mf
35
Christ en - dured the cross.
Now He sits en -
E♭
B♭
D
F sus
F
B♭
F
A

CD: 40
38
throned a - bove at the right hand of God.
Gm
E♭
Fsus
F
B♭
E♭
F
41
f
Once the suf - f'ring Ser - vant, now the King to whom we
B♭2
B♭/A
Gm7
44
bow. The Head that once was crowned with thorns is
E♭
B♭
B♭/A

47
crowned with glo - ry, crowned with glo - ry now.
Gm7
E♭2
B♭
50
CD: 41
F/A
Gm7/4
E♭2
dim.
53
LADIES unis.
accapela
mp
He tast - ed death for each of us and tri - umphed o'er the
E♭2
B♭
E♭/F
Gm
E♭
B♭/D
mp

57
cresc. poco a poco
grave.
The ho - ly Lamb has o - ver - come, His
Add MEN mp cresc. poco a poco
F sus F B♭ F/A G m
cresc. poco a poco
60
CD: 42
peo - ple shout His praise.
f
Once the suf - f'ring
E♭ F B♭ E♭ F B♭2
63
Ser - vant, now the King to whom we bow.
The
B♭/A G m7 E♭

(Without music)

NARRATOR: Jesus is crowned with glory now! He has earned His rightful place as King of kings and Lord of lords. Is there a more glorious moment in history than the moment when Satan's forces retreated, *(music begins)* sin and death were defeated, and God's redemption plan was completed? Oh, what grace . . . and what glory!

Grace in All Its Glory

NICK ROBERTSON, ALLIE LAPOINTE
and JULIA H. JOHNSTON

NICK ROBERTSON, ALLIE LAPOINTE
and DANIEL B. TOWNER
Arr. by Camp Kirkland

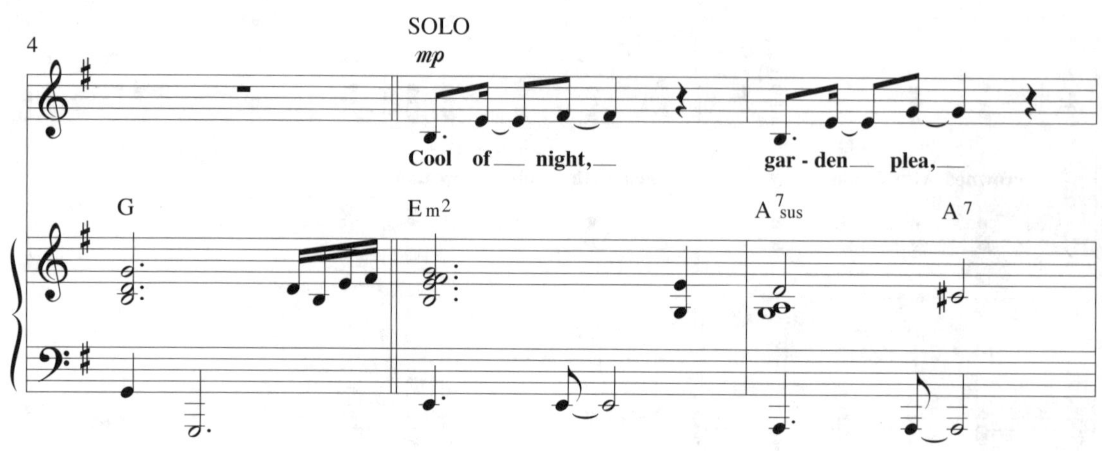

9
Fa-ther's will,
Son's de - mise,
sin-ners' stain on
Em2
A7sus
A7
Am7

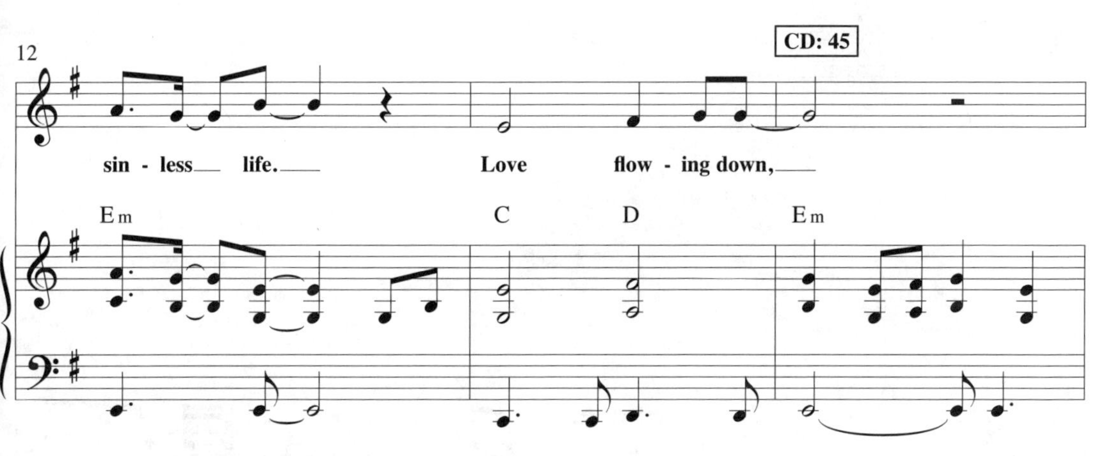
12
CD: 45
sin - less life.
Love flow - ing down,
Em
C
D
Em

15
love flow - ing down.
This was grace
C
D
Em

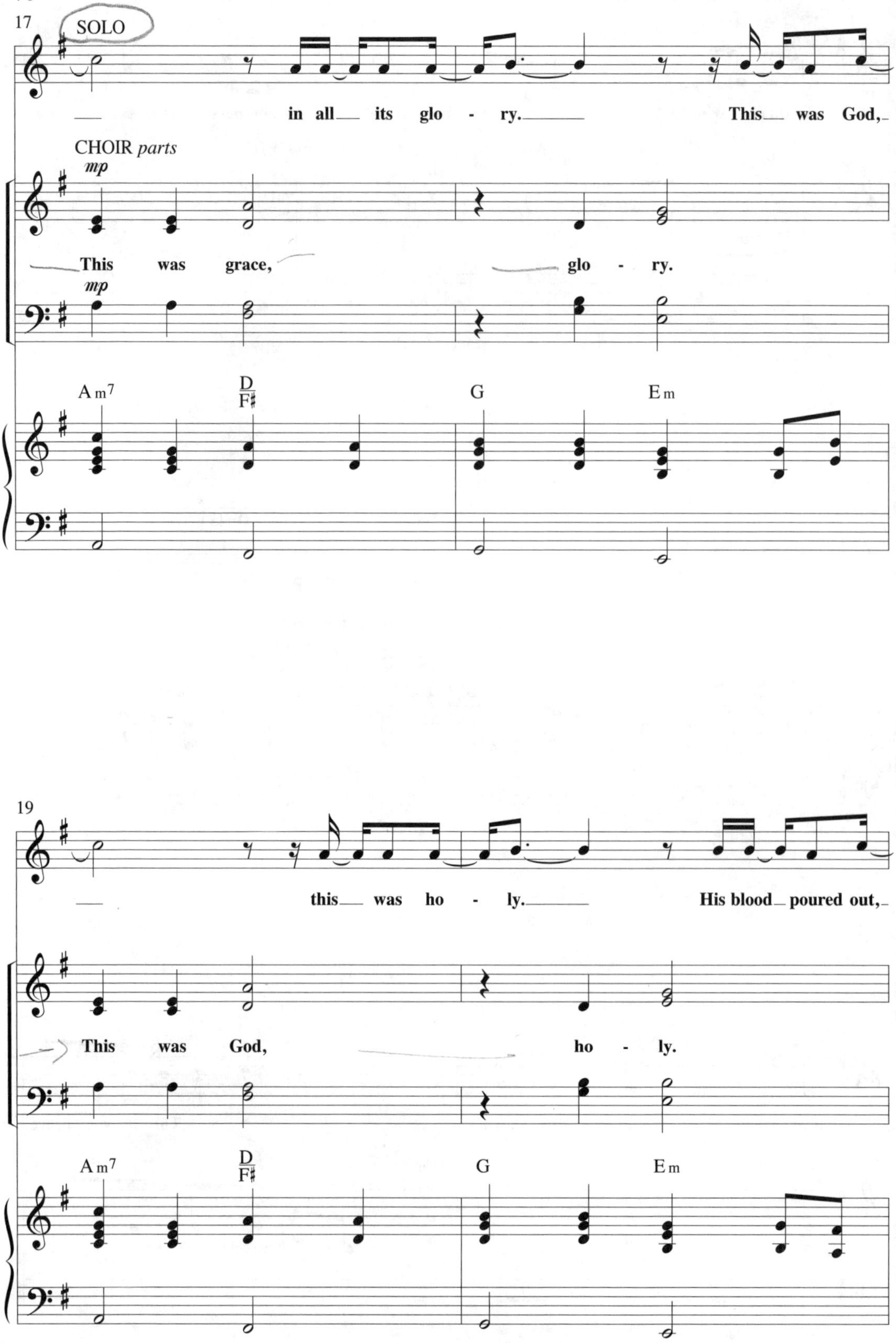

17 SOLO

in all its glo - ry. This was God,

CHOIR *parts*

mp

This was grace, glo - ry.

mp

Am7 D/F♯ G Em

21

His bod - y bro - ken for me. This was

Poured out, Oo,

C D G D/F♯ Em G/D

23

grace in all its glo - ry.

His grace.

C D C/G D/G

CD: 46
G
C/G
D/G
G
25
28
SOLO
Nail - pierced hands,
wound - ed side, a
Em2
A7sus
A7
30
crown of thorns,
for - sak - en cry.
Am7
E4/2
Em
32
Suf - f'ring Son,
an - gry crowd,
Em2
A7sus
A7

34
num - bered breaths,
si - lent now.
Am7
Em
36
CD: 47
Love flow - ing down,
love flow - ing down.
C
D
Em
C
D
39
This was grace
in all its glo -
CHOIR parts
mf
This was grace,
mf
C
E
Am7
D
F♯
mf

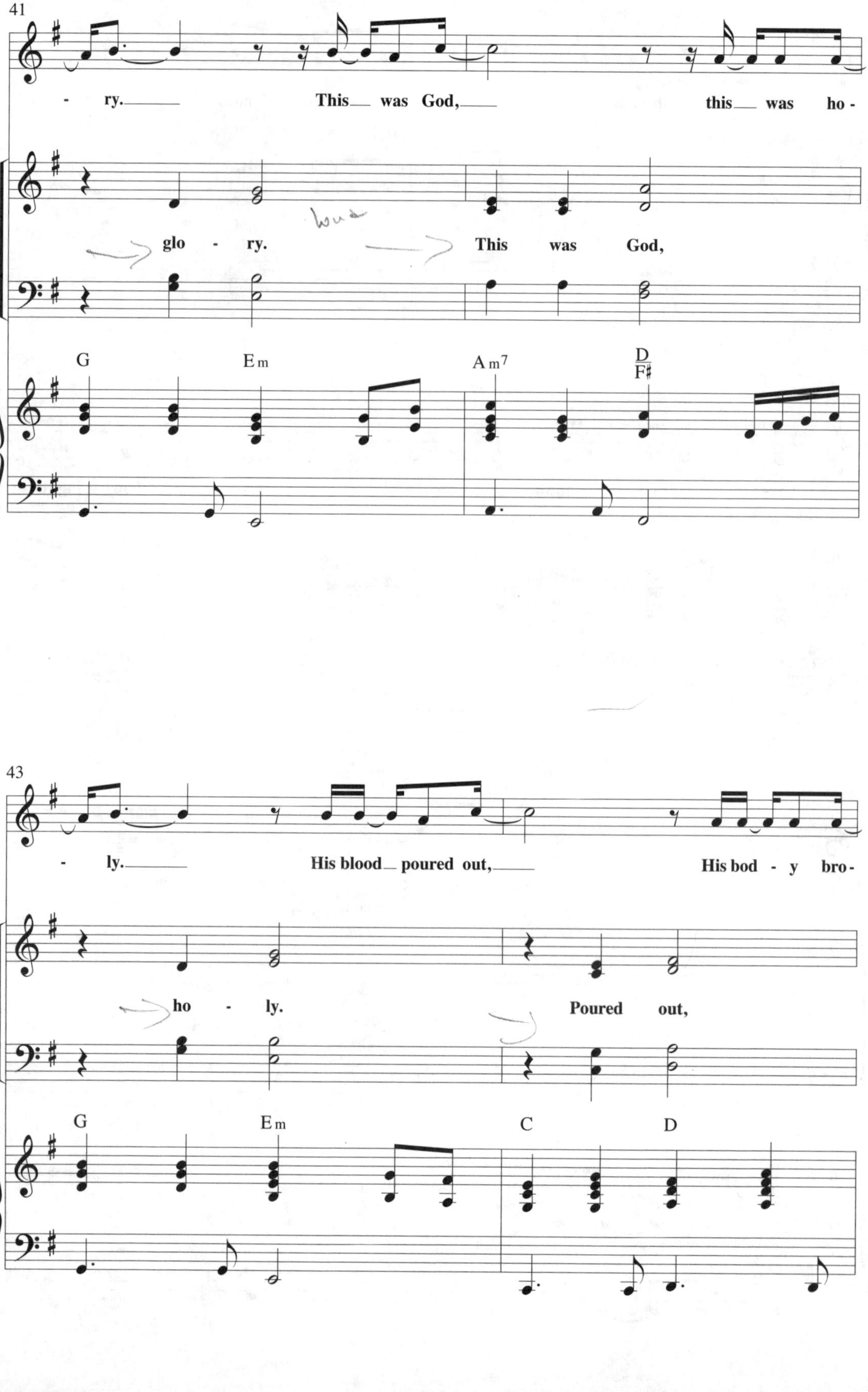

41

- ry.___ This___ was God,___ this___ was ho -

glo - ry. This was God,

G Em Am7 D/F♯

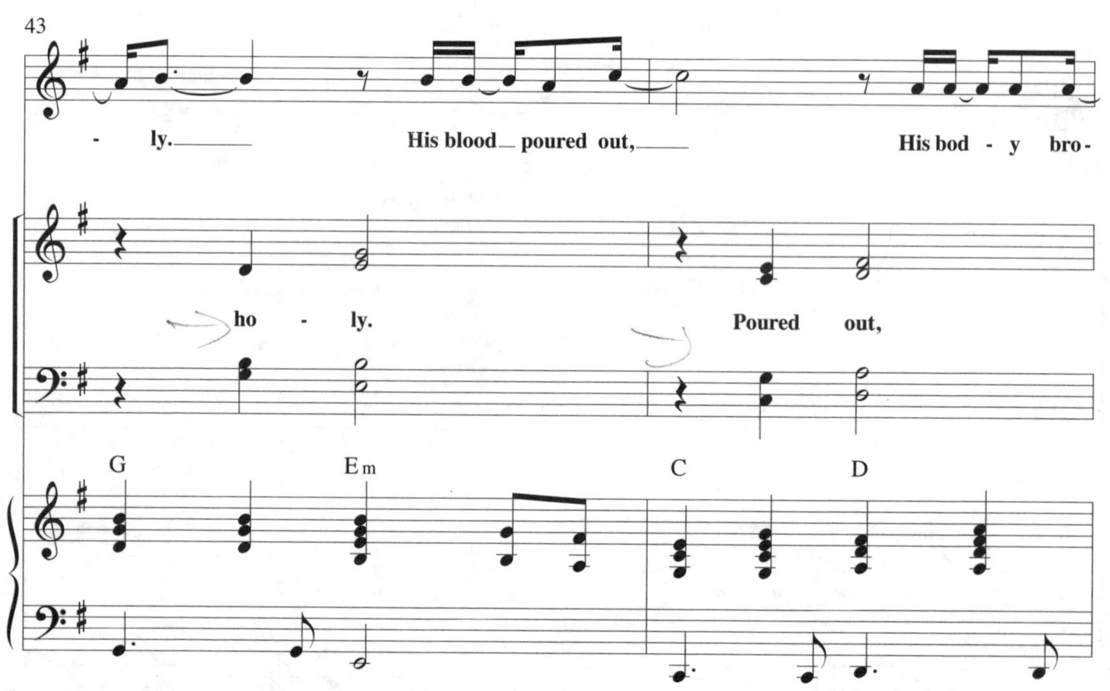

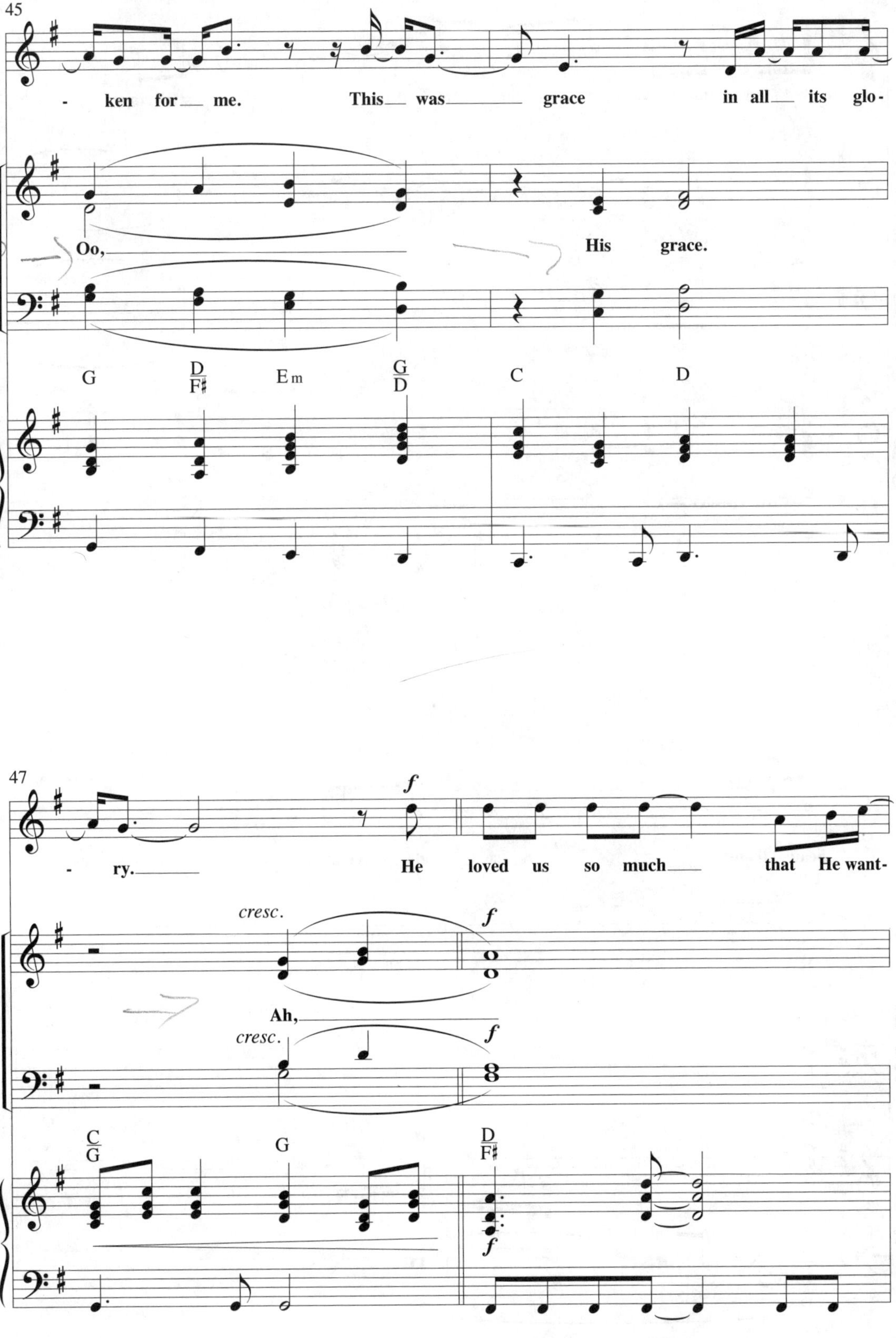

45

- ken for me. This was grace in all its glo -

Oo, His grace.

G D/F♯ Em G/D C D

49

CD: 48

- ed to give ___ a sac - ri - fice, ___ so stir - ring, so

to give, ___ Oo. ___

C/G Am7

51

dim. *sub.mp*

beau - ti - ful, ___ so glo - ri - ous. ___ This ___ was grace

C6 C

53
mp - f
in all its glo - ry.
This was God,
2nd time only
f
This was grace,
glo - ry.
f
Am7
D
F♯
G
Em
mp - f
1st time: Bass half notes on beats 1 and 3 for five measures

55
this was ho - ly.
His blood poured out,
This was God,
ho - ly.
Am7
D
F♯
G
Em

57

CD: 49 *1st time*

His bod - y bro - ken for me. This was

Poured out, Oo,

C D G D/F♯ Em G/D

59

grace in all its glo - ry. This was grace

1 (to pg. 83, meas. 53)

f

His grace.

1 (to pg. 83, meas. 53)

C D

1 (to pg. 83, meas. 53)

G

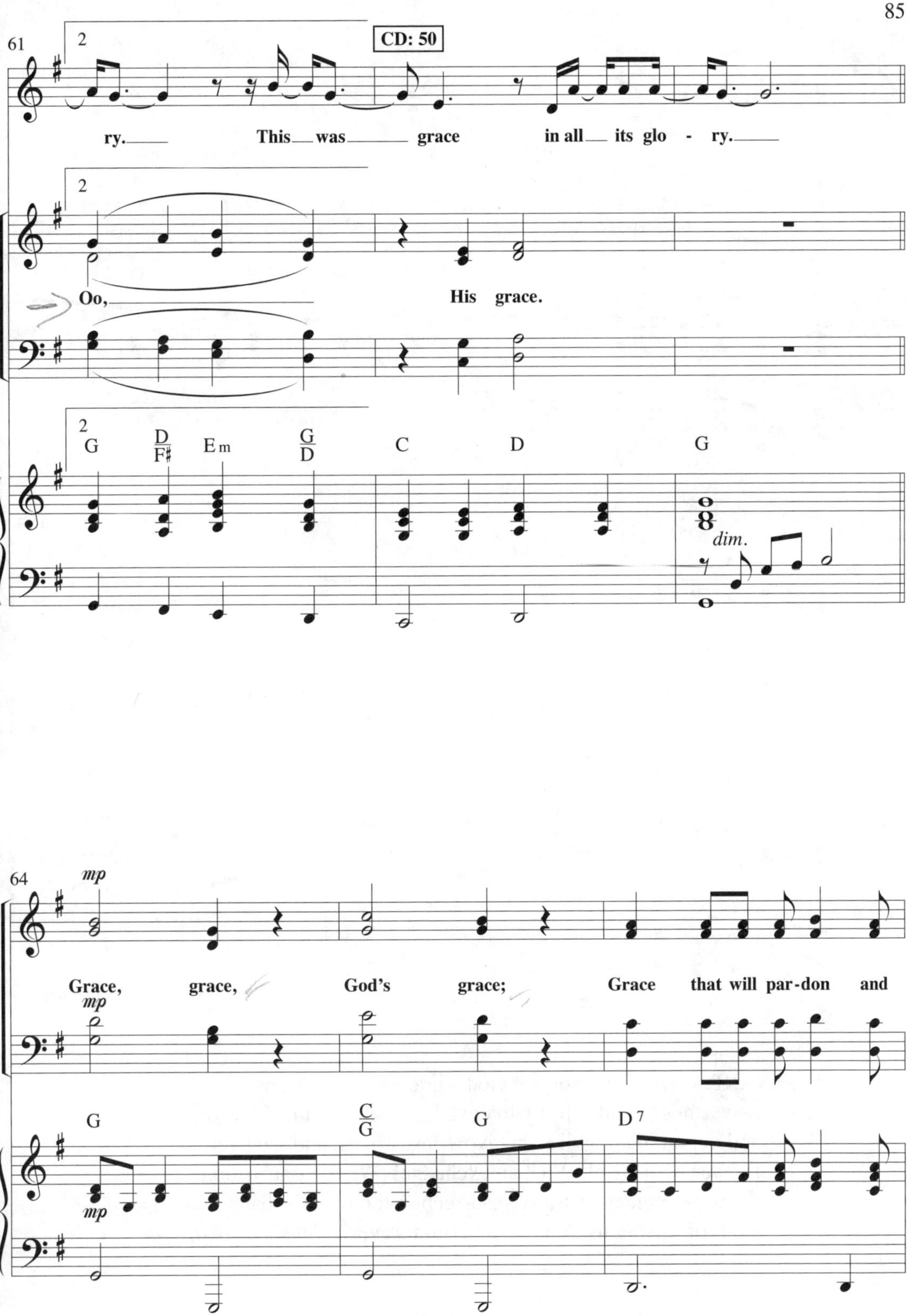

61 2 **CD: 50**

ry.___ This___ was___ grace in all___ its glo - ry.___

2

Oo,___ His grace.

2
G D/F♯ Em G/D C D G

dim.

*NARRATOR: The glory of God's grace is its greatness . . . its vastness . . . its ability to cover any and all sin. Jesus died, and our sin died with Him. Now Jesus lives, and we live forever with Him! What an exchange! What a transaction! So, as we celebrate Jesus' resurrection today, let's thank God for raising us to live with Him forever! *(Music begins)*

The King Will Rise

Words and Music by
DAVID MOFFITT,
JOHNATHAN CRUMPTON
and SUE C. SMITH
Arr. by Camp Kirkland

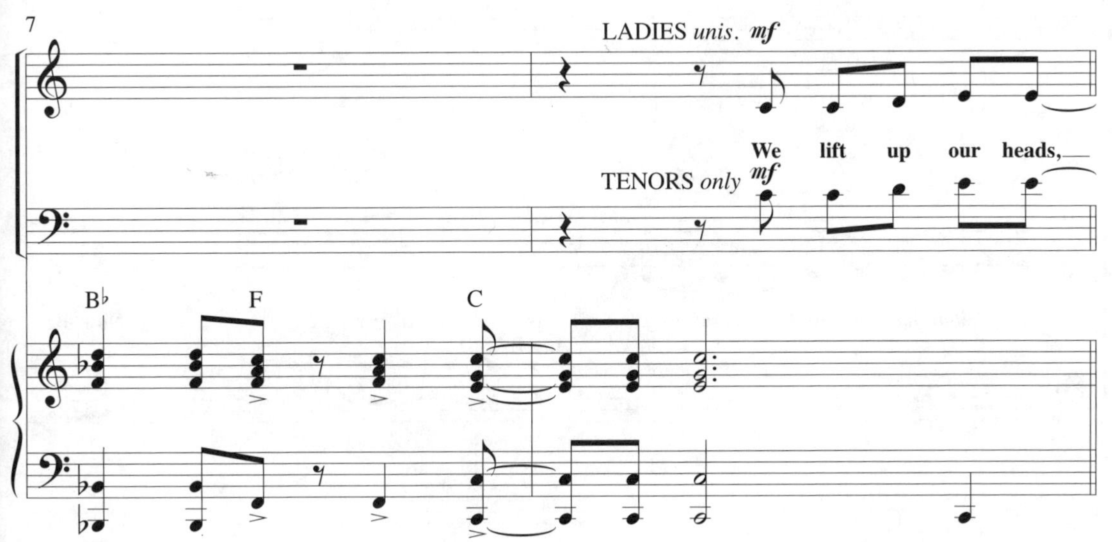

9

C

we will not be a - fraid; Our God has the pow -

11

Am7

-er to con - quer the grave. The sha - dow of night

13

FM7

C2

that has cov - ered us here Is fad - ing a - way. Now the

Add BASSES

16
morn-ing is near.
O
the dark-ness is o-
C
F
C
C
B♭
F
19
-ver.
O
C
B♭
22
CD: 52
cresc.
we wel-come the dawn.
cresc.
F
G

25
f
The King will rise, the
f
G
C
G
f
28
sov'reign and vic - to - ri - ous; The King will rise,
F
G
C
31
mag - ni - fi - cent and glo - ri - ous. He
Em7
F
G

34
writes His truth and faith - ful - ness all a - cross the skies.
Am
F
C
C/B
37
Lift up your eyes, the Morn-
Am
F
C
40
CD: 55
2nd time
2nd time to Coda
(to pg. 94, meas. 64)
- ing Sun of righ - teous - ness; The King will rise.
Em7
F
G
2nd time to Coda
(to pg. 94, meas. 64)

43
CD: 53
C
F
C
C
B♭
F
C
46
LADIES unis.
We long for the day when our faith will be sight,
TENORS only
C
48
A - mazed by His mer - cy, we'll dance in His light;
C
A m7

50
The na - tions will bow and the heav - ens will sing
Am7
FM7
52
And roll back the clouds for the King of all kings.
Add BASSES
FM7
C2
C
F
C
C
55
O the dark-ness is o - ver.
B♭
F
C

58
O
we
C
B♭
F
61
CD: 54
D.S. al Coda
(to pg. 90, meas. 26)
wel - come the dawn.
The King
G
D.S. al Coda
(to pg. 90, meas. 26)
64
CODA
mf
Here
Rise with heal - ing in
The King will rise,
mf
back to 90
CODA
C
mf

67
grad. cresc.
His wings, Rise to take His throne and pow - er.
the King will rise, the King will rise,
grad. cresc.
C B♭ C B♭
grad. cresc.
70
CD: 56
Rise up - on our songs of praise, Rise to rule and reign
the King will rise!
C B♭ C
73
for - ev - er. Rise with heal - ing in His wings,
The King will rise, the King will rise,
C B♭ C D C

76
Rise to take His throne and pow - er. Rise up - on our songs
the King will rise,
D
C
D
79
of praise, Rise to rule and reign for - ev - er.
the King will rise!
D
C
D
C
D
82
O the dark - ness is o - ver.
C
G
D

85
O we
D C G
88
CD: 57
cresc.
wel - come the dawn.
f
The King
A
cresc.
91
will rise, the sov'reign and vic - to -
D A G
f

94
- ri - ous; The King will rise, mag -
A
D
F♯m7
97
ni - fi - cent and glo - ri - ous. He writes His truth and faith -
G
A
B m
100
- ful - ness all a - cross the skies.
G
D
D/C♯
B m

CD: 58 1st time
103
Lift up your eyes, the Morn - ing Sun of righ -
G
D
F♯m7
106
1 (to pg. 97, meas. 91)
2
ff
- teous - ness; the King. The King will rise!
ff
1 (to pg. 97, meas. 91)
2
G
A
A
D
ff
109
(8)
D
(8)
8va
8vb